CHAPTER 1

THE SOLO PLAYER

Gavin, with his wide eyes full of wonder, sat in his cozy room surrounded by colorful posters of video game worlds. His fingers danced over the game controller, navigating through "Crystal Quest," his favorite game.

This game had everything Gavin loved: shiny treasures, sneaky puzzles, and big, scary monsters. But Gavin had a big challenge. He liked to play all by himself, thinking he could beat every level on his own.

One day, while playing, Gavin reached a level called the Ice Cavern. It was a slippery, sparkly world inside the game, but it was very tough. No matter how hard Gavin tried, he couldn't get past it.

He jumped, he dodged, but he always ended up falling down a slippery ice slide or getting caught by a snow monster. Gavin felt stuck. He wanted to win, but the Ice Cavern was too hard to beat alone.

CHAPTER 2

A LESSON IN THE ICE CAVERN

Sitting in the glow of his game screen, Gavin felt a mix of anger and sadness. He didn't like being stuck. It wasn't fun. Then, he saw something on the screen he hadn't noticed before—a button that said, "Invite Friends."

Gavin learned that "Crystal Quest" wasn't just for playing alone; he could invite others to join him on his adventure. He asked his parents permission before he clicked on the button and they both sat with him while he did this. Gavin pressed the "Invite Friends" button.

Soon, his screen lit up with messages from friends around his neighborhood.
They wanted to help Gavin! Together, they entered the Ice Cavern. Each friend had a special skill.

One could melt ice walls, another could fight monsters, and another could find hidden treasures. Gavin was amazed. Working together, they made a great team.

CHAPTER 3

THE POWER OF TEAMWORK

With his new friends, Gavin felt brave. They all shared ideas and helped each other. When someone got stuck, they figured it out together. Step by step, they moved through the Ice Cavern. And then, something amazing happened.

They found the Crystal
Sword, the most special
treasure in "Crystal
Quest." They had won!
Gavin learned something
very important that day.
When friends work
together, they can do big
things—bigger than
anyone can do alone.

This wasn't just a game lesson; it was a life lesson. Gavin started to see how teamwork could help in real life, like in school, playing sports, or even making a big puzzle.

CHAPTER 4

SHARING THE WISDOM

Gavin felt so happy and proud of what he had learned. He decided to write a story about his adventure. He called it "The Power of Teamwork: A Crystal Quest Adventure."

Gavin felt so happy and proud of what he had learned. He decided to write a story about his adventure. He called it "The Power of Teamwork: A Crystal Quest Adventure." He wrote about the Ice Cavern, the new friends,

and the Crystal Sword.
He even drew pictures to
go with his story.
When he was ready,
Gavin shared his story
with his class. He talked
about the game, the
challenges, and how
working together made
them strong.

His classmates listened, their eyes wide with excitement. They learned that teamwork is powerful, not just in games, but in real life too. Gavin's story made everyone want to work together more.

They saw how fun and helpful it could be. Gavin became not just a hero in "Crystal Quest" but a hero to his friends too. And from that day on, Gavin enjoyed playing games even more because he knew the best adventures were the ones shared with friends.

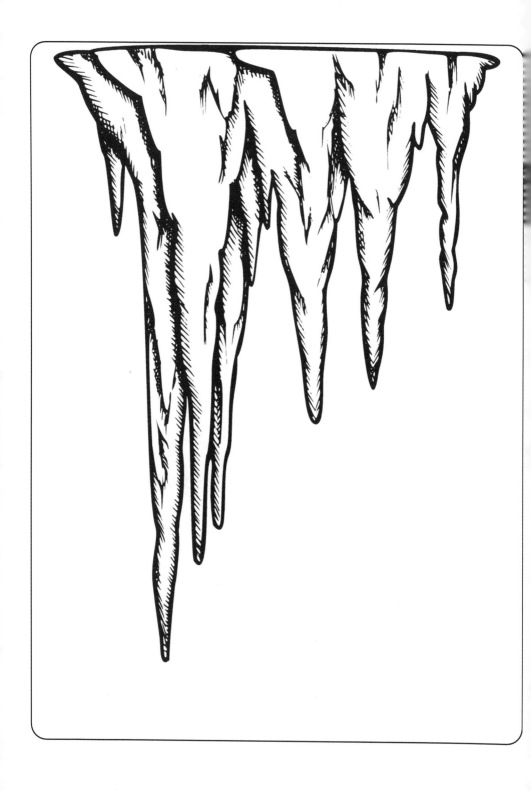

The following thoughts and questions are meant to deepen your child's understanding and appreciation of teamwork, showing them how the lessons learned in Gavin's story can be applied in their own lives.

What is Teamwork?

Ask your child what they think teamwork means. You can guide them by saying teamwork is like when Gavin and his friends worked together to beat the Ice Cavern.

Why is Teamwork Important?

Discuss why it was easier for Gavin to finish the level with friends than alone. Encourage your child to think of times when working with others helped them or could have helped them.

Different Strengths:

Talk about how Gavin's friends each had different skills that helped them succeed. Ask your child what special skills they think they have that could help in teamwork situations.